HOPE FOR WINTER

The True Story of a Remarkable Dolphin Friendship

Told by DAVID YATES, CRAIG HATKOFF, JULIANA HATKOFF, and ISABELLA HATKOFF

Scholastic Inc.

We re-dedicate this book to the millions of children around the world who struggle with disabilities of all kinds and to all children who might learn from Winter and Hope's story that through resilience, compassion, and friendship, they too can help make the world a better place for everyone.

Authors' Note: We are fortunate to have Hope's arrival at Clearwater Marine Aquarium. While these photos are not high resolution, they give us a valuable sense of the drama of this part of the extraordinary rescue as it was unfolding.

Library of Congress Cataloging-in-Publication Data is available.

ISBN 978-0-545-75037-0

10 9 8 7 6 5 4 3 2 1   14 15 16 17 18 19

Printed in the U.S.A.   88 · First printing, September 2014

Book design by Jessica Meltzer · The text was set in Garamond Three LT

We would like to thank everyone at the Clearwater Marine Aquarium and all those who helped in the rescues and rehabilitation of both Hope and Winter for their unending dedication and for sharing their stories with the world. We would like to thank Debra Dorfman, Rachel Mandel, and our mom, Jane Rosenthal. And of course we would like to thank Winter and Hope, who have become shining beacons of hope to the world.

For more information about our growing collection of true animal stories, please visit
www.owenandmzee.com, www.knut.net, www.miza.com, and www.winterstail.com.
To experience the real-life story of Winter and Hope in the new film *Winter, the Dolphin That Can,*
and for more information on Clearwater Marine Aquarium, please visit www.seewinter.com

To Our Readers,

Hope for Winter *is our twelfth children's book about remarkable animal friendships. Our first story explored an unlikely friendship between the now famous "odd couple" Owen, a baby hippo who lost his family during the Asian tsunami, and Mzee, a 130-year-old grouchy tortoise. These two animals were thrown together as a very temporary measure, but overnight formed an incredible bond that shocked the world. Similar improbable friendships have been formed between animals of all different species.*

There's one piece that remains constant in all of these unlikely friendships: each story features extraordinary animals. You may be familiar with one particularly special creature, Winter, the dolphin who lost her tail and learned to swim again. Winter's Tail *told just a portion of this dolphin's inspiring journey.* Hope for Winter *continues the story.*

In Hope for Winter, *the world's most famous dolphin faces a crisis. Dolphins are highly social animals and need a partner to remain stable. The loss of Winter's life partner, Panama, created a dilemma that could only be solved by forming a new bond with another dolphin. Then came Hope. Hope was found abandoned and alone just miles from where Winter was once discovered. The Clearwater Marine Aquarium dreamed that finding Hope would mean a solution to both dolphins' troubles. Unlike the successful overnight pairing of Owen and Mzee, this pairing would take months of planning, and the outcome was highly uncertain. We hope you enjoy reading this story about the extraordinary efforts to create a new family unit so that these two dolphins, alone, could not only survive but also thrive.*

With love and hope,

Craig Hatkoff   Juliana Hatkoff   Isabella Hatkoff

Aweak baby dolphin was discovered by a fisherman in a lagoon off the east coast of Florida. She was only a few months old and very sick. The dolphin calf was extremely dehydrated and barely breathing. Dolphins breathe air like people do, but they can't be out of the water for long periods of time, especially baby dolphins. An animal rescue team arrived and immediately decided to transport her to the Clearwater Marine Aquarium. She was placed into a small inflatable pool in the back of a van for the 165-mile journey. The mood in the van was tense. The little dolphin was dying. The rescuers didn't know if she was going to make it.

A rescue team member carries the injured dolphin.

Rescue team members carry Winter to her new home.

Exactly five years and one day earlier, another baby dolphin was swimming off the coast of Florida and got tangled in a crab trap. Her tail was badly hurt. Luckily, she was discovered by a fisherman who called a crew of rescue workers to help her. She was also brought to Clearwater. They named her Winter.

Winter survived, but eventually lost her tail. A team of experts had an incredible idea. They gave Winter a brand-new tail, called a prosthetic. Even though it was hard for her at first, Winter learned how to swim again! Now she's famous for her inspiring story. A movie was even made about Winter, called *Dolphin Tale.*

Winter with her new prosthetic tail.

When the cast and crew finished filming *Dolphin Tale*, they threw a party at Clearwater Marine Aquarium. They were happily celebrating, when they received an urgent call—a baby dolphin was on her way to the aquarium. She was very sick and might not survive the trip. A group of veterinarians, dolphin trainers, and volunteers left the party and started getting prepared. When the baby dolphin arrived, it was clear that every minute counted. The crane that was there to transfer her from the van to a tank would take too long. In order to save her life, they had to think fast. One of the rescuers, Steve McCulloch, decided to carry the baby dolphin to the tank on foot. He ran as fast as he could while holding her close in his arms. The baby dolphin was gently released into the large tank and immediately started swimming faster and faster.

Rescue team members transport the baby dolphin to a tank.

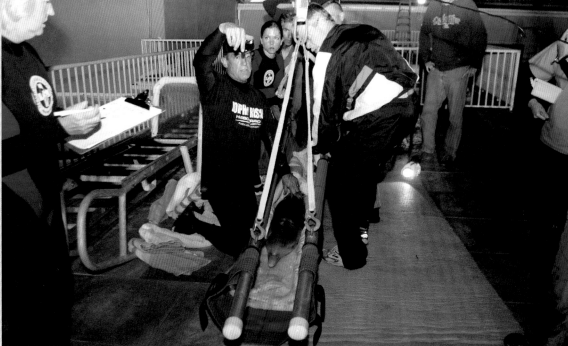

Steve stood in the tank with Abby Stone, the head dolphin trainer, and Juli Goldstein, a veterinarian. The baby's speed swimming was not a good sign. Juli gave her a quick examination. The little dolphin was in critical condition—her heart rate was too high and she was extremely dehydrated. The speed swimming was a sign of distress. The three could hardly breathe while waiting to see what the little dolphin would do next. After a few frightening minutes, the baby started to swim more slowly, but the team knew they had to give her something to drink right away.

Clearwater workers help the baby dolphin adjust to her tank.

A trainer bottle-feeds the little dolphin.

In the wild, baby dolphins drink milk from their mother until they are about two years old. Without the baby's mother to feed her, the trainers put a fish milk shake in a baby bottle and offered it to the little dolphin. She didn't know what to do with it at first, but eventually started drinking.

The trainers were relieved, but had to feed the baby every two hours to keep her alive. The Clearwater Marine Aquarium team examined her every day by checking her weight and listening to her heart. Slowly, the little dolphin started to recover.

The team at Clearwater decided it was too dangerous to release the baby dolphin back into the wild. She wouldn't be able to feed herself and she didn't have the survival skills that she would have learned from her mother. The aquarium was going to be her new home.

But what should they call the little dolphin? The aquarium asked the public for suggestions. Out of hundreds of entries, one name stood out above all others . . . Hope.

Hope was getting stronger and stronger every day. She moved from her tank to an aboveground pool. She had fun playing with hoops and swimming with the trainers. She started jumping as high as she could out of the pool and loved splashing around. Her favorite water toy was a squirt gun!

A trainer works with Hope.

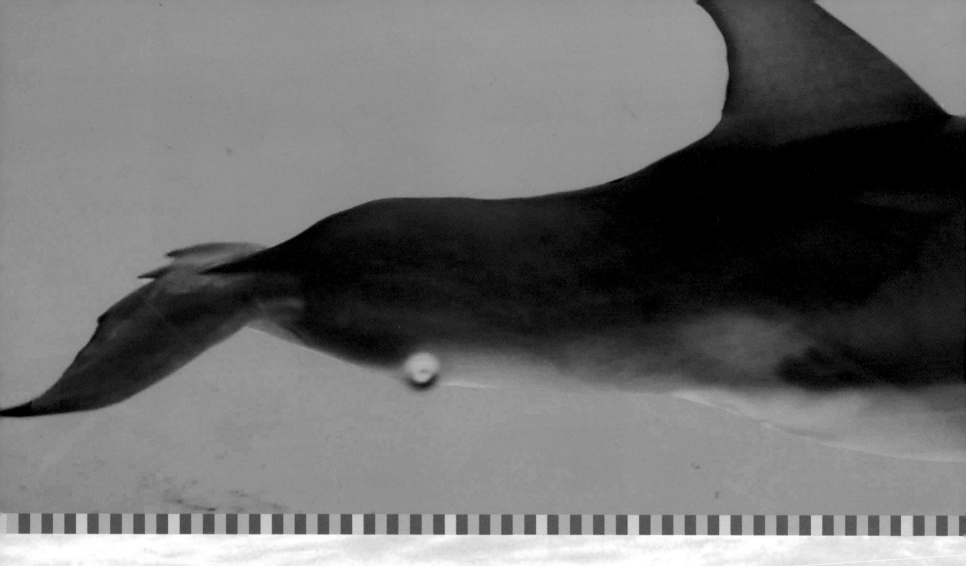

About a year and a half after Hope arrived at Clearwater, the trainers decided it was time for her to meet the other dolphins at the aquarium—Panama and Winter. Dolphins like to live with other dolphins, just like human families do. Panama was about thirty-five years old, which was old for a dolphin, and much older than five-year-old Winter. Panama had become like a grandmother to Winter.

They spent most of their time together. Sadly, the trainers didn't know how much longer Panama would be around. They were worried because Winter shouldn't live alone. She has to be with another dolphin so she can stay happy and healthy. Could Hope be the companion for Winter that they had been waiting for?

Hope and Panama meet for the first time.

Hope was just a baby when she was rescued and had never been around other dolphins. The trainers were nervous—would they all get along? Would Hope recognize Winter as a dolphin with her prosthetic tail? Would Panama and Winter accept Hope into their family?

As the gentler, older dolphin, who had already welcomed Winter, Panama was introduced to Hope first. The trainers had worried for nothing. The meeting was a success! Panama and Hope hit it off immediately and it didn't take long before Panama became like a grandmother to Hope, too. But, the trainers still wondered, how was Winter going to react?

Hope and Winter are fast friends.

Hope and Winter pose for the camera.

Hope and Winter proved the trainers had no reason for concern. After spending just a few minutes together, Hope and Winter were fast friends. Winter soon became like a teenage big sister to Hope. Hope became a playful little sister to Winter. They eat, play, swim, and have lots of fun together. Their favorite game is tug-of-war. Winter and Hope act just like human siblings do. The large tank at the aquarium has three gates, one for each dolphin. Sometimes Winter would block Hope from going through her gate. It's as if she was saying—stay out of my room! But Panama was always there to keep her little dolphins in line.

The three dolphins had tons of fun together, but Panama was growing older. Then she fell very ill. The trainers and veterinarians did everything they could to help her, but she wasn't getting better. The moment everyone at the aquarium was dreading had come. Panama was gone. Sadness filled the Clearwater team. Winter and Hope both had already lost their mothers. Now they had lost their grandmother, too. The trainers didn't know if the bond between Winter and Hope was strong enough. Would they be able to get along without Panama? After days of tense observation, the worrying was over. Winter and Hope were going to be fine because they had each other.

Happy moments with Hope, Winter, and Panama.

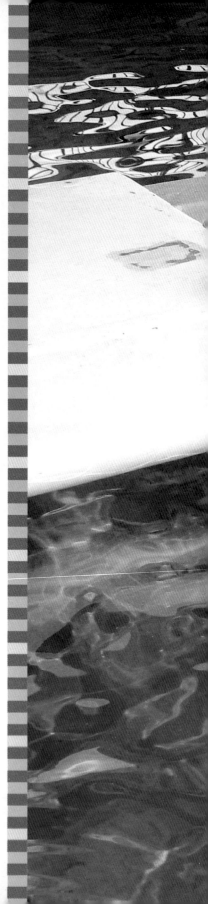

Winter and Hope show off their skills.

Today, Winter and Hope are more than fine. They are happy and healthy living at the aquarium together. They have the best trainers, veterinarians, and volunteers taking care of them. Large crowds of kids and families come to visit them every day. They come to see Winter, the dolphin with the prosthetic tail, and her best friend, Hope. They come to see the little dolphins who have inspired people around the world with their bravery, strength, and special friendship.

Clearwater Marine Aquarium
www.SeeWinter.com

Founded in 1972, the Clearwater Marine Aquarium (CMA) is the world's most recognized marine life rescue center, dedicated to the rescue, rehabilitation, and release of injured, sick, or stranded marine life. This nonprofit organization, located in Clearwater, Florida, educates residents, visiting tourists, and millions more around the world via its global media presence on the importance of protecting and preserving our waters and marine life. CMA also oversees the area's sea turtle nesting program, combing miles of beaches during nesting season to ensure nests are located and cared for, and that hatchlings safely make it to the water. CMA staff and volunteers are on call 24/7 to rescue stranded or injured sea turtles, dolphins, river otters, and more.

Once an animal arrives at CMA's hospital, a team of experienced staff biologists, veterinarians, and volunteers create a rehabilitation plan for the animal, catering to its specific injuries or illnesses. Sometimes, as with Winter and Hope, the injuries are so severe that the animal would not survive on its own in the wild and therefore cannot ever be released. CMA works with agencies such as the National Marine Fisheries and the Florida Fish and Wildlife Conservation Commission to make these decisions. If an animal is unable to be released back into its natural environment, it becomes a lifelong resident of the Clearwater Marine Aquarium.

In spite of its tremendous growth and global presence, CMA remains a "neighborhood" aquarium, a place where children and adults alike can visit anytime to wonder at the unending diversity, grace, and beauty of the creatures of the sea. Environmental education plays an important role in the aquarium's marine life outreach. In addition to sharing their expertise and amazing animal rehabilitation stories, staff and volunteers work diligently to teach people how they can help protect marine animals from injuries. CMA conveys this important message through a variety of hands-on educational opportunities, including eco-boat tours, kids' camps, tours, off-site presentations, and animal interactions. CMA's wide-screen theater provides guests with films and behind-the-scenes footage of animal rescues, rehabilitation, and release.

Chief Executive Officer David Yates began working at CMA in February 2006. In a short period of time, his leadership propelled the aquarium to places it had never been. As the former CEO of the Ironman Triathlon, he has extensive experience in innovative thinking and leading people. Mr. Yates facilitated and managed the intensive process of helping Winter get a prosthetic tail. Yates produced the new film *Winter, the Dolphin That Can* that recounts the real-life story of both Winter and Hope, which can be found at seewinter.com.

Amazing similarities between Winter and Hope:

- Winter and Hope are both female Atlantic bottlenose dolphins who were rescued, rehabilitated, and now live permanently at the Clearwater Marine Aquarium.

- Winter and Hope were the same age when rescued–about two months old.

- Hope was found very close to the spot where Winter was found in Florida–only about fifteen miles away.

Hope was discovered exactly five years and one day after Winter had been found.

The same rescue worker who found Hope was also a primary rescuer for Winter.

Hope spent one year in an aboveground pool that had been built specially for *Dolphin Tale*. Without the movie, there wouldn't have been a place outside for Hope before the trainers could introduce her to Panama and Winter.

Dolphin Facts:

- There are more than forty different kinds of dolphins. Bottlenose dolphins, like Panama, Winter, and Hope, are the most common.

- Bottlenose dolphins are found in warm waters and tropical oceans around the world.

- Dolphins might look like fish, but they are actually mammals, just like humans.

- Bottlenose dolphins can grow to be ten to fourteen feet long and weigh up to 1,100 pounds.

- Dolphins breathe through a blowhole in the top of their head.

- Bottlenose dolphins can jump up to sixteen feet in the air!

- Dolphins eat mainly fish, but also eat squid and shrimp.

- Dolphins are very social and swim together in groups called pods. Up to fifteen bottlenose dolphins can live together in a group.

- Bottlenose dolphins can swim up to eighteen miles an hour through the water.

- Dolphins hunt for food by using clicking sounds, called echolocation. The clicking sounds bounce back from an object, or prey, telling the dolphin about its size, shape, and location.

- Dolphins use clicks and whistles to communicate with one another.

- Dolphins have been known to come to the aid of injured dolphins and even humans!

Eyes closed it's her entirely
Paul Eluard, "In exile."

So we shall recount what a true night is.
An enchanted, free night. A night for all nights.
A woman for all women.
Yes, right: a lesson of the night.
Philippe Sollers, "Le cavalier du Louvre"

An Enchantment
Christian Durieux

WITHDRAWN

For f

To *the memory of my father, to my mother.*

To Jean-Marc and Véronique, Valérie
and Laurent, Laurence and Yves, lovely people.

To those who, in their own way, also made this book:
Sébastien, Fabrice, Patrice, Fabien,
Celia, Didier, Evelyne, Elise, Claude, Alain.

And a big thanks to Chrystel, queen of photo editing.

WHAT IMBECILES, GOOD GOD!

WHAT IMBECILES.

GOOD GOD, ALL THOSE PREGNANT WOMEN'S DRESSES! WHAT AN ERA.

AH! BERTAUT...HE'S VERY MUCH IN HIS ELEMENT.

AND DE LA MOTTE, MAGNIFICENT!

THEY'RE PERFECT! THEY TAKE TO THIS LIKE DUCKS TO WATER.

IT'S THEIR CROWNING MOMENT THIS EVENING, NOT MINE.

11

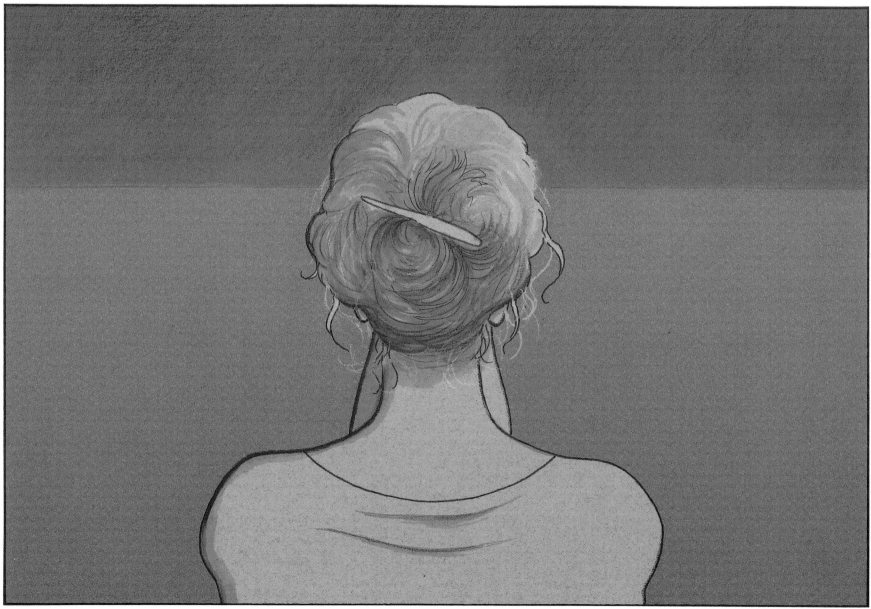

HE DIDN'T SEE YOU.

THE GUARD DIDN'T SEE YOU. I'M THE ONE HE'S SEARCHING FOR. YOU HAVE A FUNNY WAY OF HIDING.

I'M NOT HIDING.

SORRY?

YOU'RE NOT WITH THEM BACK THERE?

I DON'T THINK I KNOW YOU. I CAN'T KNOW EVERYONE.

19

20

21

22

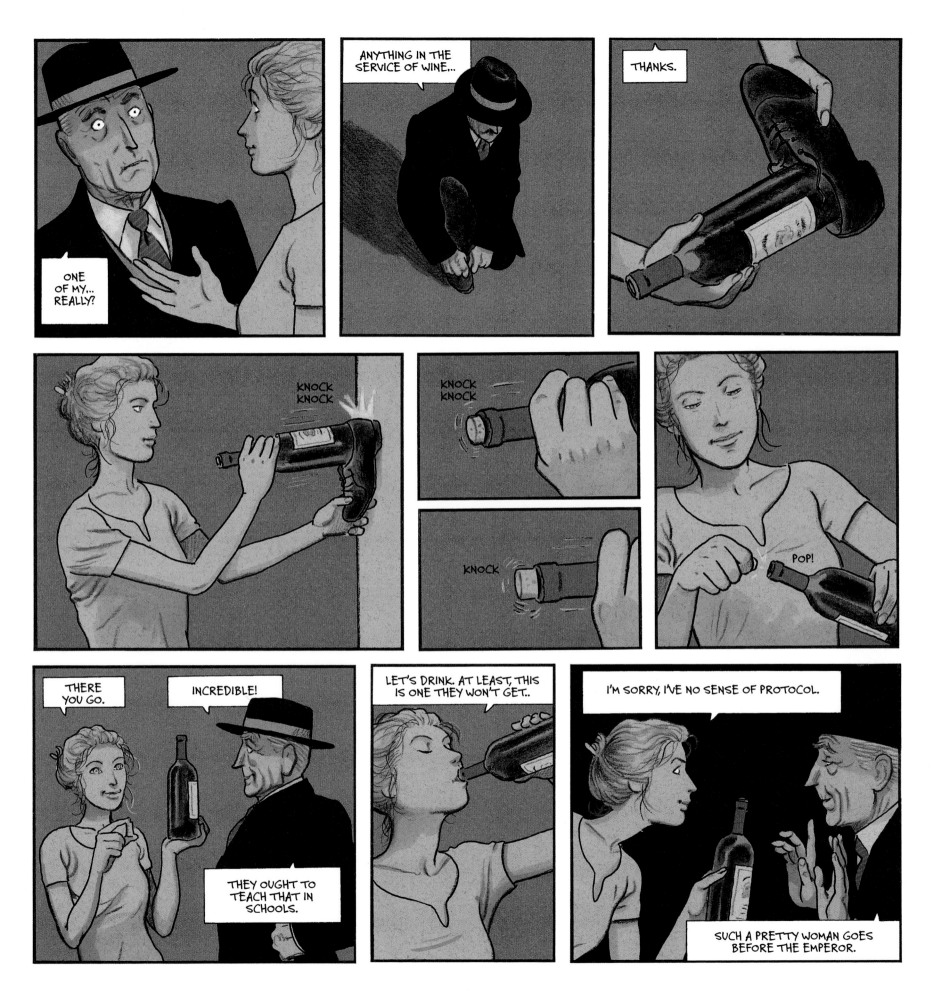

25

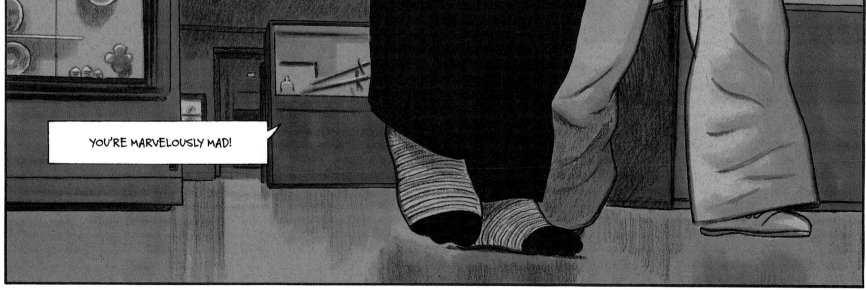

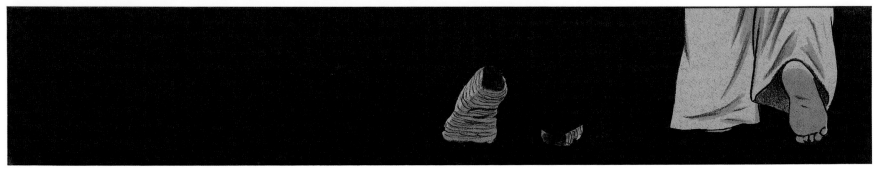

YOU KNOW, YOU DON'T MAKE IT TO MY POSITION JUST LIKE THAT. THERE WERE TWISTS AND TURNS. I WAS EVEN A CABINET MINISTER ONCE.

A LONG TIME AGO. LONG BEFORE YOUR BIRTH.

BEFORE MY BIRTH! YOU'RE EXAGGERATING.

AT A TIME, IN ANY CASE, WHEN THE MUSEUM WASN'T JUST A MUSEUM.

MY OFFICE WAS BEHIND THIS DOOR. THE OFFICES OF THE MINISTRY OF FINANCE!

AND...I WAS THE MINISTER OF FINANCE.

CAFÉ RICHELIEU

34

37

38

43

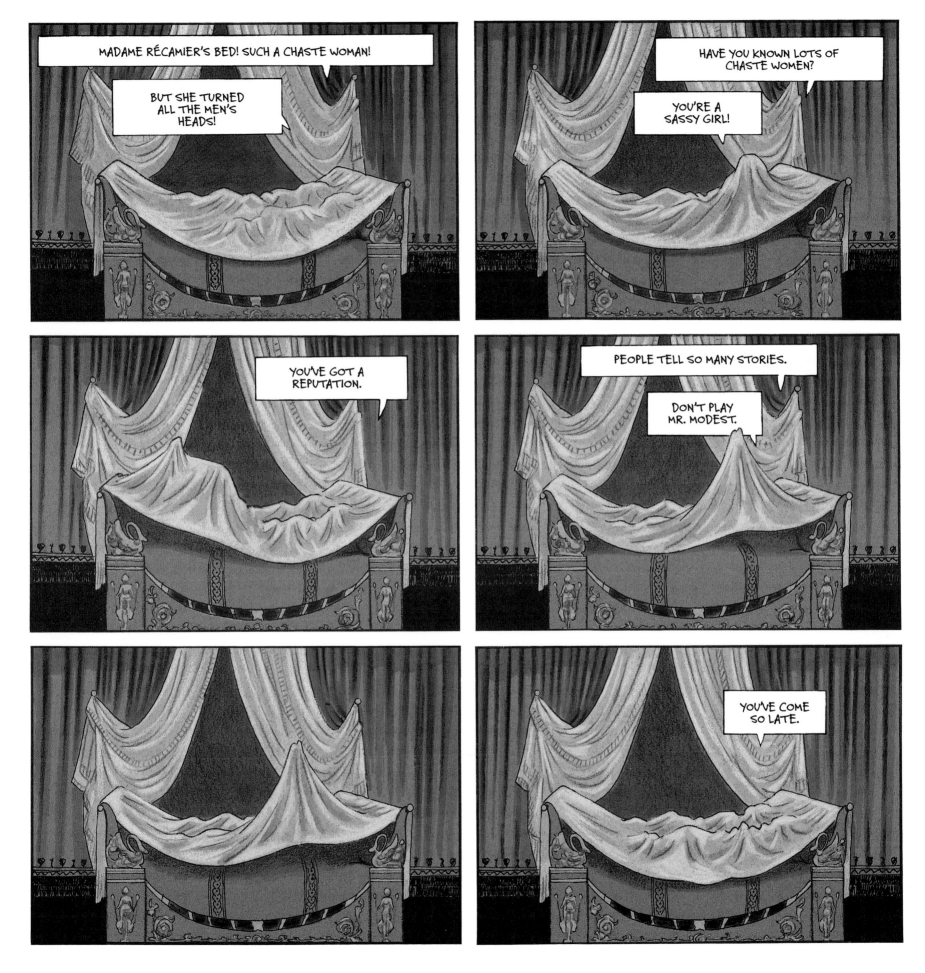

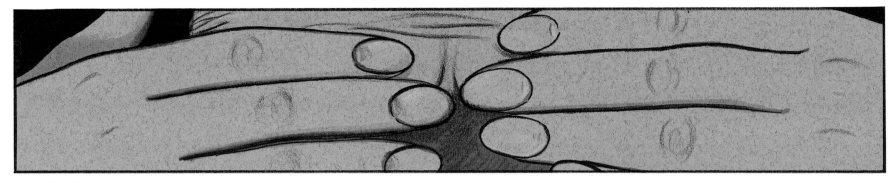

ARE YOU DREAMING, MILORD?

MMM.

I SEE.

FRAGONARD NEVER IS TIRESOME, IS HE?

NEVER!

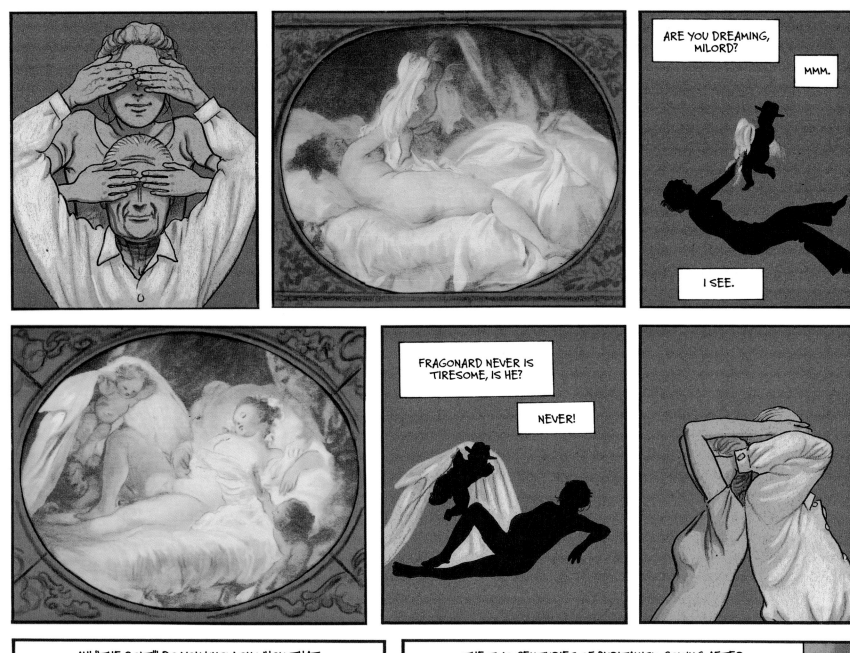

AH! "THE BOLT"! DO YOU KNOW ON WHOM THAT IMPETUOUS LOVER IS CLOSING THE DOOR? —HM?

THE TWO CENTURIES OF PURITANISM COMING AFTER THEM! HE'S PROTECTING THEIR VOLUPTUOUSNESS.

56

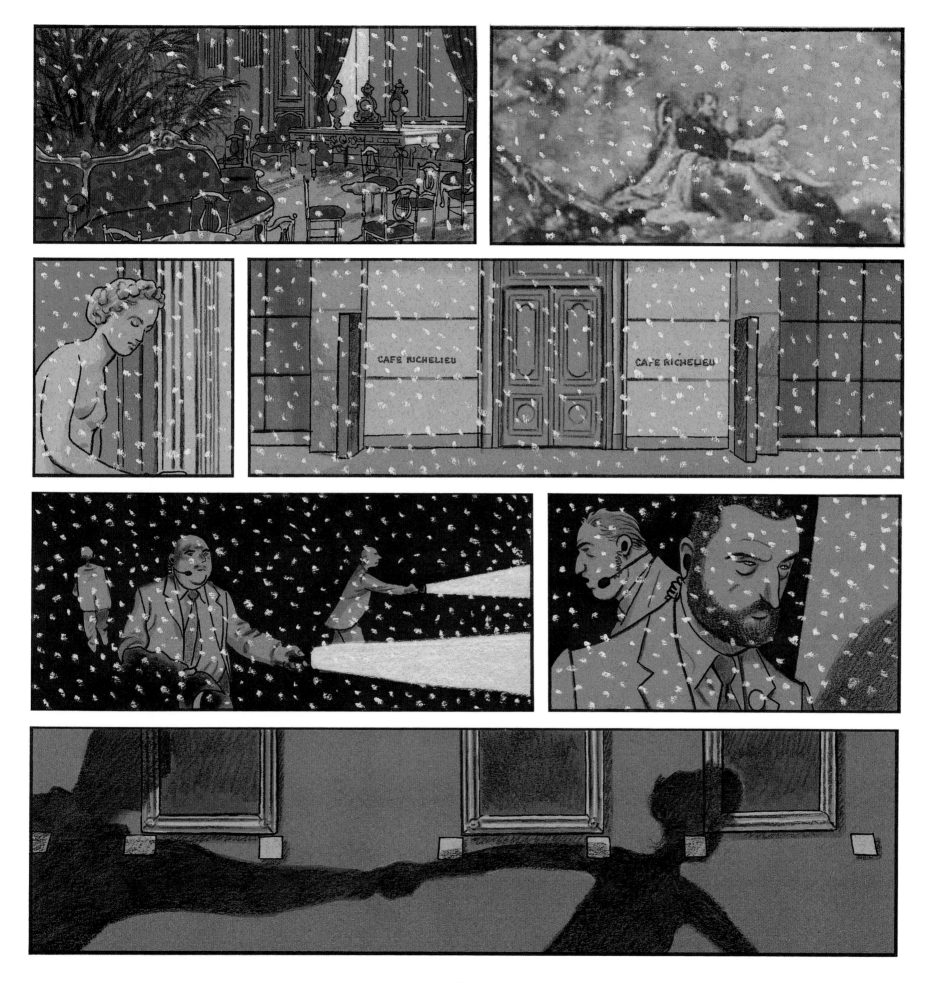

"THE EMBARKATION FOR CYTHERA"...
THE MARVELOUS WATTEAU.

APHRODITE'S ISLAND...
THE ISLE OF LOVERS.

60

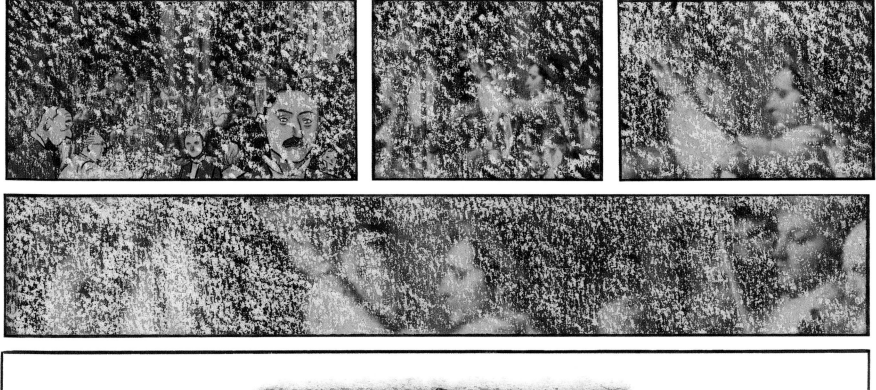

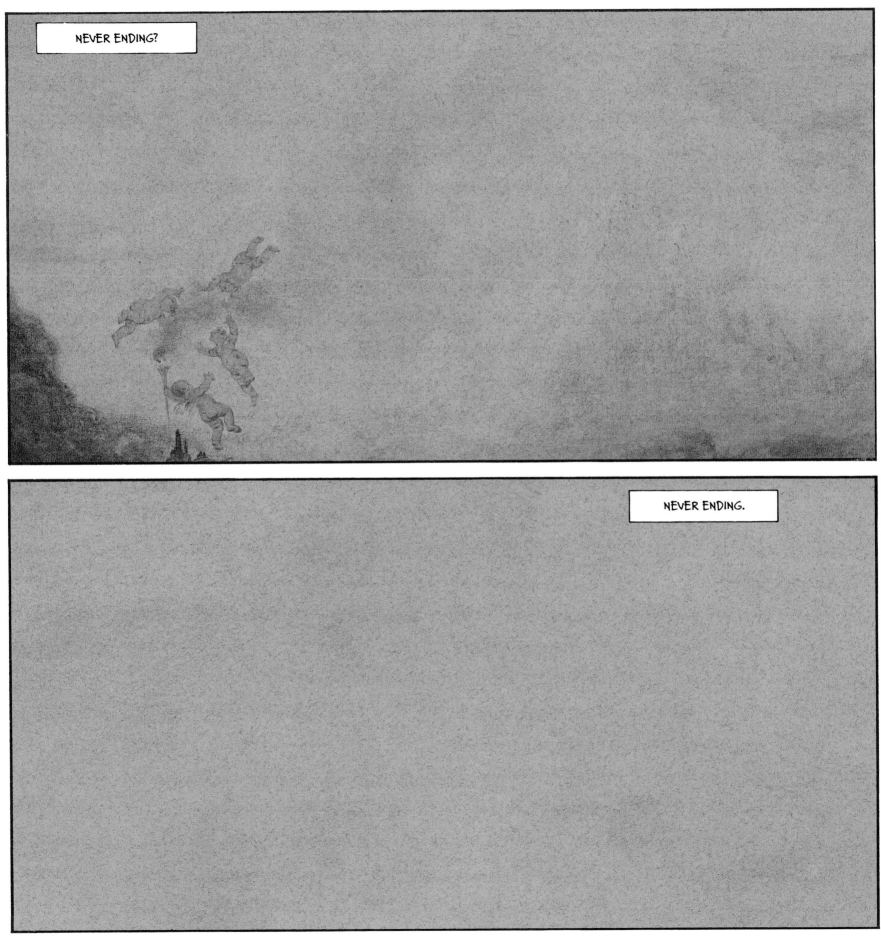

NEVER ENDING?

NEVER ENDING.

To love museums, you must love ghosts

At the Louvre, there is the ghost of Leonardo and that of Mona Lisa, but also the ghost of Francis I, who bought the Gioconda, and of Vincenzo Perugia, the glazier who stole it in 1911. There are the ghosts of the Greeks massacred at Scio and of the plague victims of Jaffa and of Delacroix who painted their suffering, there are the ghosts of Nazi boots. The Louvre is bestirred by silent movements, rustlings, tears, and hidden smiles. And there is the "fête gualante", the garden party, the ghost of Watteau and those of its actors.

Antoine Watteau died in 1721, well before the French Revolution, well before the other century. He was only 37 years old and he will remain the painter of the "fête galante." It has been said elsewhere that the Royal Academy created this genre for him especially when, in 1717, he presented the painting which gained him reception into that grand institution: The Pilgrimage to Cythera. It may be only a legend but no matter.

With Watteau, a gentle wind breathes through the Louvre, that of Zephyrs who, according to Hesiod, transported the young goddess of Love, Aphrodite, to the isle of Cythera. With Watteau, an enchanted world, elegant, delicate, melancholic too, traverses the Louvre's rooms. You dream that, beneath the ample folds, her step barely brushes the soil. The actors are blurry. The garden party is a theater, you're there, but you're hiding, women are often shown from behind, in the distance. They must be divined. You must see them under their napes.

In Watteau's paintings, there's the landscape, and mythology isn't far away either, but there's the intimate, the intimacy of two bodies seeking one another, whispering to one another. When I dreamt of the Louvre to create a story about it, I dreamt of intimacy in that grand theater décor. Great museums are like great cities: seen from without, their grandeur impresses, from within they are villages, minuscule patches where a personal adventure can spring up and spread its wings. And I dreamt of this great, intimate adventure in that grand décor.

My imagination is homespun. It has little tolerance for special effects, they're too much for it. Amid the Louvre, strolling its halls, I can only gather up small things, piece them together in my manner, naively, composed of odds and ends basically, and try to conjure up a fragile, gentle, vivid moment. I make the world like a small spectacle on my own scale, where one dances while finding one's steps, where the roles are exchanged: who's leading whom on this night which is a pilgrimage, a fête galante made for only two people?

The night concludes at the embarkation for the isle of Cythera. A gentle voyage. But the voyage is also a departure and you cannot stop yourself from casting a final glance over your shoulder towards what you've accomplished, or haven't. Jean Cocteau, whom I love, classified the entirety of his disparate works under the heading of poetry: poetry of theater, poetry of the novel, poetry of cinema, critical poetry or of the quotidian. Quite naively, I'd like to create a poetry of comic books.

Christian Durieux

List of works
selected by the author, in order of appearance.

Musée du Louvre

Henri Loyrette
President and Director

Hervé Barbaret
General Administrator

Juliette Armand
Head of Cultural Development

Violaine Bouvet-Lanselle
Head of the Publishing Service,
Office of Cultural Development

Publishing
Series Editor
Fabrice Douar
Publishing Service,
Office of Cultural Development,
Musée du Louvre

Acknowledgments at the Musée du Louvre

Henri Loyrette, Hervé Barbaret,
Juliette Armand, Marie-Catherine Sahut,
Violaine Bouvet-Lanselle,
Fanny Meurisse, Diane Vernel,
Adrien Goetz, Laurence Castany,
Christine Fuzeau, Camille Sourisse,
Ariane Rabenou, Nelly Girault
Chrystel Martin, Virginie Fabre,
Caroline Damay, Morgane Ramain,
Nastasia Raymond, Zahia Chettab,
Valérie Coudin, Catherine Dupont.

To Nathalie Trafford, Denis Curty,
Thierry Masbou, Christophe Duteil,
Emmanuel Hoffman, Cécile Bergon,
Béatrice Hedde, Anne Grandadam,
Marc Giner for their invaluable

Also available in the Louvre collection:
Glacial Period, $14.95
On the Odd Hours, $14.95
The Sky Over the Louvre. $19.99
Rohan at the Louvre, $19.99

P&H: $4 1st item, $1 each addt'l.

See previews and more at
www.nbmpub.com

We have over 200 titles,
write for our color catalog:
NBM
160 Broadway, Suite 700, East Wing,
New York, NY 10038

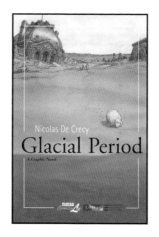

ISBN 978-1-56163-705-8
Library of Congress Control Number: 2012950214
© Futuropolis/Musée du Louvre éditions 2011
© NBM 2013 for the English translation
Translation by Joe Johnson
Lettering by Ortho
1st printing February 2013 in Singapore

Verlaine poem "Cythere' on p.60 translated by Bergen
Weeks Applegate in Paul Verlaine: His Absinthe-tinted
Song, a Monograph On the Poet, With Selections From His
Work. Chicago: R. F. Seymour, The Alderbrink press, 1916.

Comicslit is an imprint
and trademark of

NANTIER · BEALL · MINOUSTCHINE
Publishing inc.
new york